A CHRISTMAS CAROL: 12 AQA GCSE ENGLISH LITERATURE A STAR EXAM ANSWERS

Full mark A Star (Grade 9) Answers

By Joseph Anthony Campbell

CONTENTS

THE QUALITY CONTROL SYSTEM™ OR HOW TO GET AN A STAR!

The Quality Control System™ is fourfold.

It involves:

1) An efficient summary of the examination paper.

2) A concise focus upon the Assessment Objectives in the exam and how to approach them.

3) Clear instructions on your timings and how long you should spend on each question. ***This is the most important point of fact in this fourfold system***.

4) Further to point 3, the approximate word count per mark you should be consistently aiming for in each minute of your exam.

My students have applied all of the techniques of the Quality Control System™ I am providing you with to gain A stars (Grade 9's) in their examinations. You can replicate them by following the advice in this book. Following these rules has ensured success for my students in English Literature and their other subjects and it will do for you too! The Quality Control System is explained more fully at the end of this book.

CHANGES TO THE 2022 AQA ENGLISH LITERATURE GCSE

Because of the impact of the Coronavirus pandemic, there are some changes to the 2022 AQA English Literature GCSE exams.

There is 1 hour 40 minutes (100 minutes) for the Paper 1 exam (unless you have extra time). In the 2022 examinations, this paper has a total of 60 marks.

Paper 1 is divided into 3 sections: You will be doing **two** of the following options:

Paper 1N. 19th-century novel – 1 item. 30 marks (AO1, AO2, AO3)
We are looking in this book at this '**19th-century novel**' section and the '**A Christmas Carol**' option. There are 12 examples of Grade 9, A star essays in this book. There will be one question on each nineteenth century novel. In each question there will be a short, extract from the novel and you will be required to widen your response to the novel as a whole.

Paper 1M. Modern prose/drama – 1 item. 30 marks (AO1, AO2, AO3).

Paper 1P. Anthology of poetry – 1 item. 30 marks (AO1, AO2, AO3)

The following 12 questions and answers will help you to prepare your grade 9 essays and to massively improve your practice for your exams as I have covered all of the major characters in '**A Christmas Carol**' in this book and all of the major themes.

The best approach for a **Grade 9** is to spend 50 minutes on each question; 40 minutes writing and 10 minutes making notes, planning and checking your final answer for basic corrections at the end of the examination.

A CHRISTMAS CAROL FIRST ESSAY – EBENEZER SCROOGE

Read the following extract from Chapter 1 and then answer the question that follows.

In this extract Scrooge is being introduced to the reader.

External heat and cold had little influence on Scrooge. No warmth could warm, nor wintry weather chill him. No wind that blew was bitterer than he, no falling snow was more intent upon its purpose, no pelting rain less open to entreaty. Foul weather didn't know where to have him. The heaviest rain,
5 and snow, and hail, and sleet, could boast of the advantage over him in only one respect. They often 'came down' handsomely, and Scrooge never did. Nobody ever stopped him in the street to say, with gladsome looks, 'My dear Scrooge, how are you? When will you come to see me?' No beggars implored him to bestow a trifle, no children asked him what it was o'clock, no
10 man or woman ever once in all his life inquired the way to such and such a place, of Scrooge. Even the blindmen's dogs appeared to know him; and when they saw him coming on, would tug their owners into doorways and up courts; and then would wag their tails as though they said, 'No eye at all is better than an evil eye, dark master!'
15 But what did Scrooge care? It was the very thing he liked. To edge his way along the crowded paths of life, warning all human sympathy to keep its distance, was what the knowing ones call 'nuts' to Scrooge.

Starting with this extract, how does Dickens present Scrooge as an outsider to society?

Write about:

• *how Dickens presents Scrooge in this extract*
• *how Dickens presents Scrooge as an outsider to society in the novel as a whole.*

[30 Marks] (AO1 = 12; AO2 = 12; AO3 = 6)

(50 Minutes Total = 40 Minutes Writing + 10 Minutes Reading Extract/Making Notes/Planning)

(600 Words Maximum per Essay = 15 Words per Minute)

Dickens presents and describes Scrooge in this extract as an outsider to society. Dickens uses language to draw us into the story and to present the character of Scrooge. This is achieved through the use and effect of imagery such as the weather, "No warmth could warm, nor wintry weather chill him." Dickens's language is highly descriptive and creates a vivid sense of how Scrooge is unaffected by the weather, "External heat and cold had little influence on Scrooge." The listing of the types of weather that have no effect on Scrooge i.e., "The heaviest rain, and snow, and hail, and sleet," demonstrate how he is presented as almost being outside of the natural world and the weather it creates, as Scrooge's nature is set. Dickens goes on to describe how Scrooge is cut off from his fellow humans within the natural world and how no one ever asks, "My dear Scrooge, how are you?". Scrooge is presented as being completely outside of society and as "warning all human sympathy to keep its distance", that at this point in the novella, "it was the very thing he liked."

Dickens presents Scrooge as.an outsider to society in the novel as a whole through Scrooge's interactions. For example, when he refuses his nephew Fred's invitation for Christmas dinner in the first stave, he responds with a now oft quoted and grumpy

"Bah!" followed by "Humbug!" He also dismisses his nephew as he imparts the season's greetings with a frosty "Good afternoon,". He then callously replies to two charity collectors that if the poor cannot go to prison or the workhouses and that "If they would rather die," that "they had better do it, and decrease the surplus population". Scrooge hoards his money, perhaps through fear and this expresses itself in a lack of care for the needs of others as exemplified in the line, "...as the clerk came in with the shovel, the master predicted that it would be necessary for them to part." Thus, he will not allow Bob Cratchit to have more coal and remains an 'outsider', in that he is unable to share what he has. Dickens uses a strong narrative voice that is, "standing in the spirit at your elbow" and when initially introducing Scrooge states, "Oh! But he was a tight-fisted hand at the grindstone, Scrooge!" The use of 'Oh!' and the exclamatory mark that follows, illustrate the excessive levels of Scrooge's miserliness. This is heightened through Dickens use of a simile to describe Scrooge, as "Hard and sharp as flint". However, as the novella progresses, there is a sharp contrast between Scrooge here and in the later part of the novella. As the "Spirits" show him others enjoying being in one another's company and sharing on Christmas Day and of how he himself once enjoyed this, he becomes redeemed and transformed from a miserly, isolated man to a generous and kind member of society.

Dickens presents Scrooge throughout the novella as the central, pivotal character that drives the plot. He also uses various examples, throughout the novella, to heighten and emphasise the point that greed and isolation has a profoundly negative influence on Scrooge and those around him. As an outsider, Scrooge is socially isolated and eschews societal expectations of courtesy and politeness and is cut off deliberately from the friendliness and warmth of others. This would be perceived as ungentlemanly in Victorian times and the emblematic redemption and transformation of Scrooge at the end of the novella would have been appreciated by Dickens' contemporary readers and it is similarly appreciated by modern readers today.

(600 words)

A CHRISTMAS CAROL SECOND ESSAY – FRED: SCROOGE'S NEPHEW

Read the following extract from Chapter 1 of <u>A Christmas Carol</u> and then answer the question that follows.

In this extract Fred visits Scrooge.

"But why?" cried Scrooge's nephew. "Why?"

"Why did you get married?" said Scrooge.

"Because I fell in love."

"Because you fell in love!" growled Scrooge, as if that were the only one thing in the
5 world more ridiculous than a merry Christmas. "Good afternoon!"

"Nay, uncle, but you never came to see me before that happened. Why give it as a
reason for not coming now?"

"Good afternoon," said Scrooge.

"I want nothing from you; I ask nothing of you; why cannot we be friends?"

10 "Good afternoon," said Scrooge.

"I am sorry, with all my heart, to find you so resolute. We have never had any quarrel,
to which I have been a party. But I have made the trial in homage to Christmas, and
I'll keep my Christmas humour to the last. So A Merry Christmas, uncle!"

"Good afternoon," said Scrooge.

15 "And A Happy New Year!"

"Good afternoon," said Scrooge.

His nephew left the room without an angry word, notwithstanding. He stopped at the outer door to bestow the greetings of the season on the clerk, who cold as he was, was warmer than Scrooge; for he returned them cordially.

Starting with this extract, how does Dickens present Scrooge's nephew Fred?

Write about:

• *how Dickens presents Fred in this extract*
• *how Dickens presents Fred in the novel as a whole.*

[30 Marks] (AO1 = 12; AO2 = 12; AO3 = 6)

(50 Minutes Total = 40 Minutes Writing + 10 Minutes Reading Extract/Making Notes/Planning)

(600 Words Maximum per Essay = 15 Words per Minute)

Fred is the son of Fan, Scrooge's late sister and the nephew of Scrooge. Prior to this extract, Scrooge has refused a Christmas dinner invitation from his nephew. Dickens conveys Fred's insistence to have Scrooge attend through the use of bold questions, "'But why?' cried Scrooge's nephew. 'Why?'". The repetition of the word 'why' reinforces Fred's complete lack of understanding as to why Scrooge will not attend Christmas dinner with him; the sole remaining member of his family. Scrooge's resulting question has a sarcastic tone, "Why did you get married?". From this point in the extract, there is a marked contrast between Fred and Scrooge's length of speech and the precision of Scrooge's speech suggests he is determined to conclude the conversation, "'Good afternoon,' said Scrooge." In this extract, Scrooge repeats the words 'Good afternoon,' four times.

Dickens presents Fred in this extract as a considerate, thoughtful man who has no agenda, "'I want nothing from you; I ask nothing of you; why cannot we be friends?'" Dickens conveys the clear and discernible differences in the attitude and behaviour of Scrooge and Fred. Fred maintains his positivity despite Scrooge's brusque and impatient attitude. "'I'll keep my Christmas humour to the last. So A Merry Christmas, uncle!'" Fred's positive, non-reactive and forgiving nature is presented by Dickens through Fred's dialogue, "'I am sorry, with all my heart, to find you so resolute. We have never had any quarrel, to which I have been a party.'" And in the way he "...left the room without an angry word, notwithstanding" thus, maintaining his equanimity, positivity and enthusiasm. The placing of this conversation early on in the novella indicates its key significance as the plot develops.

Dickens presents Fred in the novel as a whole, as a cheerful and kind man. He offers unconditional generosity to Scrooge. Being kind, he embodies the spirit of Christmas. Dickens uses language to draw us into his story and he uses a strong narrative voice. The narrator states, "...for it is good to be children sometimes, and never better than at Christmas, when its mighty Founder was a child himself" as Fred celebrates Christmas with his friends. Dickens presents Fred as diametrically opposed to Scrooge in his attitude and behaviours as Fred is able to fully enjoy and partake of childish pleasures at Christmas and he enjoys the company of his friends. Fred also demonstrates persistence and compassion concerning Scrooge, as he states to his friends with conviction, that he will invite his Uncle Scrooge to Christmas dinner each year, "...whether he likes it or not, for I pity him." His concern and unconditional support are revealed through both his pity and his persistence. In the final stave, when Scrooge finally turns up for Christmas dinner, Fred welcomes him wholeheartedly. "Let him in! It is a mercy he didn't shake his arm off." Fred's enthusiasm is evident here.

Dickens uses the character of Fred to show the importance of compassion. Fred endears himself to the readers through both his words and actions. Dickens uses Fred to influence the plot's development and he is present before and after Scrooge's transformation as the novella progresses. He is an effective character in the story and persistent in his cheerful approach to Christmas and in his kindness and compassion with both Scrooge and Bob Cratchit. The character of Fred would have been appreciated by Dickens contemporaries as he remains a gentleman despite Scrooge's ungentlemanly conduct and disparagement of his marriage. A contemporary and modern reception would consider Fred's Christmas spirit to demonstrate the finest qualities of a kind and compassionate human being.

(600 words)

A CHRISTMAS CAROL THIRD ESSAY – MARLEY'S GHOST

Read the following extract from Chapter 1 of <u>A Christmas Carol</u> and then answer the question that follows.

In this extract Scrooge is visited by Marley's Ghost.

Again the spectre raised a cry, and shook its chain and wrung its shadowy hands.

"You are fettered," said Scrooge, trembling. "Tell me why?"

"I wear the chain I forged in life," replied the Ghost. "I made it link by link, and yard by yard; I girded it on of my own free will, and of my own free will I wore it. Is

5 its pattern strange to you?"

Scrooge trembled more and more.

"Or would you know," pursued the Ghost, "the weight and length of the strong coil you bear yourself? It was full as heavy and as long as this, seven Christmas Eves ago. You have laboured on it, since. It is a ponderous chain!"

10 Scrooge glanced about him on the floor, in the expectation of finding himself surrounded by some fifty or sixty fathoms of iron cable: but he could see nothing.

"Jacob," he said, imploringly. "Old Jacob Marley, tell me more. Speak comfort to me, Jacob!"

"I have none to give," the Ghost replied. "It comes from other regions, Ebenezer

15 Scrooge, and is conveyed by other ministers, to other kinds of men. Nor can I tell you what I would. A very little more is all permitted to me. I cannot rest, I cannot stay, I cannot linger anywhere. My spirit never walked beyond our counting-house—mark me!—in life my spirit never roved beyond the narrow limits of our money-changing hole; and weary journeys lie before me!"

20 It was a habit with Scrooge, whenever he became thoughtful, to put his hands in his breeches pockets. Pondering on what the Ghost had said, he did so now, but without lifting up his eyes, or getting off his knees.

Starting with this extract, explore how Dickens uses the ghosts to help Scrooge change his attitudes and behaviour.

Write about:

• *how Dickens uses Marley's Ghost in this extract*
• *how Dickens uses the ghosts to help Scrooge change his attitudes and behaviour in the novel as a whole.*

[30 Marks] (AO1 = 12; AO2 = 12; AO3 = 6)

(50 Minutes Total = 40 Minutes Writing + 10 Minutes Reading Extract/Making Notes/Planning)

(600 Words Maximum per Essay = 15 Words per Minute)

Dickens steadily increases the dramatic tension prior to this extract as Scrooge has a vision of his door knocker bearing the face of his old business partner, Jacob Marley. In this extract, Scrooge is visited at home by Marley's ghost, seven years after his death. The ghost is frightening for Scrooge and Dickens states that it "shook its chain" and "wrung its shadowy hands". Scrooge finds the courage to speak, despite his "trembling". "You are fettered,", Scrooge asks the ghost. Dickens was affected by seeing 'fettered' prisoners on his travels and perhaps draws on this experience in his writing here. Scrooge also becomes visibly afraid as Dickens states that "Scrooge trembled more and more."

Marley's chains are a symbol of the greed and the self-interest that he demonstrated in life and they are also used by Dickens as a metaphorical message that serves to make Scrooge aware of the fate that awaits him in the afterlife. Marley states to Scrooge that his "coil ...was full as heavy and as long as this, seven Christmas Eves ago." And that Scrooge has "laboured on it, since." And then states with finality, "It is a ponderous chain". Marley later instructs Scrooge that he has but one single chance to avoid the same fate: that he will be visited by "Three Spirits" and that he must heed their message. Dickens' placing of this conversation early in the novella suggests its key significance as the plot unfolds.

Dickens uses the 'Spirits' to help Scrooge change his attitudes and behaviour in the novel as a whole. When Scrooge is first visited by the gentle but commanding "Ghost of Christmas Past", Scrooge is reluctant yet instructed by the "Spirit" with the imperatives, "Rise! and walk with me!". Later, when observing Belle, his former fiancé, Dickens writes, "'Remove me.' Scrooge exclaimed,' I cannot bear it.'" And later states that Scrooge "...wrestled" with the 'Ghost of Christmas Past'. However, when Scrooge meets the exuberant and expressive "Ghost of Christmas Present" and later observes the acutely ill Tiny Tim, he is stung by his own words, that he spoke in the first stave, which are repeated back to him by the Spirit, "If he be like to die, he had better do it, and decrease the surplus population." Thus, Scrooge is "overcome with penitence and grief." This is a clear demarcation of the beginning of Scrooge's transformation. By the time Scrooge meets the "Ghost of Christmas Yet to Come" he has become aware that it's "...purpose is to do me good," and he follows it with "a thankful heart." He finally declares that he "...will live in the Past, the Present, and the Future. The Spirits of all Three shall strive within me." Thus, his transformation is complete.

During the time that Dickens wrote his book there was a tradition of reading and telling ghost stories at Christmas, and the structure of the three ghosts representing the ghosts of Christmas "Past", "Present" and "Future" appeals to readers. The number three is also particularly significant in traditional tales and stories. Dickens' language draws the reader into the story and presents characters and scenes that are entertaining through the abrupt shifts from comedy to tragedy and the contrast of light and dark throughout the novella. The dramatic context of the "Three Spirits" would also have been greatly enjoyed during Dickens time and his themes of justice and mercy combined with elements of the gothic genre have proved popular contemporarily. Ultimately, the 'Three Spirits' present Dickens' metaphorical message and completely change Scrooge's behaviour and attitudes which then leads to his transformation and redemption.

(600 words)

By Joseph Anthony Campbell

A CHRISTMAS CAROL FOURTH ESSAY – THE GHOST OF CHRISTMAS PAST

Read the following extract from Chapter 2 of <u>A Christmas Carol</u> and then answer the question that follows.

In this extract, Scrooge meets the Ghost of Christmas Past for the first time.

It was a strange figure – like a child: yet not so like a child as like an old man, viewed through some supernatural medium, which gave him the appearance of having receded from the view, and being diminished to a child's proportions. Its hair, which hung about its neck and down its back, was white as if with age; and yet the face had not a wrinkle

5 in it, and the tenderest bloom was on the skin. The arms were very long and muscular; the hands the same, as if its hold were of uncommon strength. Its legs and feet, most delicately formed, were, like those upper members, bare. It wore a tunic of the purest white, and round its waist was bound a lustrous belt, the sheen of which was beautiful. It held a branch of fresh green holly in its hand; and, in singular contradiction of that

10 wintry emblem, had its dress trimmed with summer flowers. But the strangest thing about it was, that from the crown of its head there sprung a bright clear jet of light, by which all this was visible; and which was doubtless the occasion of its using, in its duller moments, a great extinguisher for a cap, which it now held under its arm.

Even this, though, when Scrooge looked at it with increasing steadiness, was not its
15 strangest quality. For as its belt sparkled and glittered now in one part and now in another, and what was light one instant, at another time was dark, so the figure itself fluctuated in its distinctness: being now a thing with one arm, now with one leg, now with twenty legs, now a pair of legs without a head, now a head without a body: of which dissolving parts, no outline would be visible in the dense gloom wherein they melted
20 away. And in the very wonder of this, it would be itself again; distinct and clear as ever.

Starting with this extract, how does Dickens present The Ghost of Christmas Past in A Christmas Carol?

Write about:

• *how Dickens presents The Ghost of Christmas Past in this extract*
• *how Dickens presents The Ghost of Christmas Past in the novel as a whole.*

[30 Marks] (AO1 = 12; AO2 = 12; AO3 = 6)

(50 Minutes Total = 40 Minutes Writing + 10 Minutes Reading Extract/Making Notes/Planning)

(600 Words Maximum per Essay = 15 Words per Minute)

Dickens presents and describes the "Ghost of Christmas Past" in this extract. There is a build-up of tension before the dramatic and structurally significant moment of the ghost's appearance. The 'Ghost of Christmas Past' is the first spirit to visit Scrooge as Marley's ghost predicted. Dickens' language is highly descriptive and he repeatedly uses contrast to convey the duality and seeming contradictions of the 'Ghost'. Dickens states, through the narrative voice, that the 'Ghost' is "delicately formed" and that the "tenderest bloom was on the skin", yet it has "uncommon strength". Dickens also uses imagery such as "purest white" and that from the "...crown of its head there sprung a bright clear jet of light," yet it has "a great extinguisher for a cap". The apparition is also described as "a strange figure" appearing to be both "...like a child: yet not so like a child as like an old man". In this extract, an example that Dickens uses that heightens and emphasises the contradictory and dualistic nature of the 'Ghost' is found in the lines, "It held a branch of fresh green holly in its hand; and, in singular contradiction of that wintry emblem, had its dress trimmed with summer flowers". It is also described by Dickens as being an ephemeral spirit, presenting different perceptions, through constantly revealing itself and disappearing; "...what was light one instant, at another time was dark, so the figure itself fluctuated in its distinctness." The 'Ghost' is surreal, flickering like candlelight and perhaps Dickens is presenting the idea of the possibility of redemption from one's past actions.

Dickens presents 'The Ghost of Christmas Past' in the novel as a whole as gentle, taciturn yet commanding. Its' contradictory nature is consistently presented throughout the novella. The 'Ghost' is calm and gentle in the way it communicates with Scrooge. "The Spirit gazed upon him mildly. Its gentle touch, though it had been light and instantaneous, appeared still present to the old man's sense of feeling." Dickens use of the words 'mildly' and 'gentle' demonstrate the kind, well-meaning nature of the 'Ghost'. The 'Ghost' is also taciturn, answering Scrooge's questions with a precision of speech, stating that it is here for "Your welfare!" to Scrooge. Seemingly in contradiction with these former qualities, the 'Ghost' is also commanding, stating, "Rise! and walk with me!" Both of these imperative commands are accentuated by exclamatory remarks and this forceful, commanding, phrasing suggests strength which is reminiscent of Dickens' description of the ghost's 'uncommon strength' in the extract. The use of the ghost's language highlights the power dynamic between the 'Ghost' and Scrooge which is shown through the line, "'What.' exclaimed the Ghost, 'would you so soon put out, with worldly hands, the light I give'".

Dickens uses the 'Spirits' to help Scrooge change his attitudes and behaviour in the novel as a whole. The structure of the three ghosts, showing the past, present and future, appeals to readers. The contrast of light and dark acts as an intertwining metaphor that creates dramatic irony throughout the novella. During the time that Dickens wrote 'A Christmas Carol' there was a tradition of reading and of telling ghost stories at Christmas. The dramatic context and spectacle of the supernatural would have been enjoyed during the time of Dickens. This may also highlight contextual differences in terms of potentially different reactions over time as belief in ghosts may be less widespread in a modern context than at the time Dickens wrote the novella. In this novella, the "Ghost of Christmas Past" is ultimately presented by Dickens, as a pivotal character that drives the plot.

(600 words)

A CHRISTMAS CAROL FIFTH ESSAY – THE GHOST OF CHRISTMAS PRESENT

Read the following extract from Chapter 3 of <u>A Christmas Carol</u> and then answer the question that follows.

In this extract, Scrooge meets the Ghost of Christmas Present for the first time.

In easy state upon this couch, there sat a jolly Giant, glorious to see; who bore a glowing torch, in shape not unlike Plenty's horn, and held it up, high up, to shed its light on Scrooge, as he came peeping round the door.

"Come in!" exclaimed the Ghost. "Come in! and know me better, man!"

5 Scrooge entered timidly, and hung his head before this Spirit. He was not the dogged Scrooge he had been; and though the Spirit's eyes were clear and kind, he did not like to meet them.

"I am the Ghost of Christmas Present," said the Spirit. "Look upon me."

Scrooge reverently did so. It was clothed in one simple green robe, or mantle, bordered

10 with white fur. This garment hung so loosely on the figure, that its capacious breast was bare, as if disdaining to be warded or concealed by any artifice. Its feet, observable beneath the ample folds of the garment, were also bare; and on its head it wore no other covering than a holly wreath, set here and there with shining icicles. Its dark brown curls were long and free; free as its genial face, its sparkling eye, its open hand, its

15 cheery voice, its unconstrained demeanour, and its joyful air.

Girded round its middle was an antique scabbard; but no sword was in it, and the ancient sheath was eaten up with rust.

"You have never seen the like of me before!" exclaimed the Spirit.

Starting with this extract, how does Dickens present the Ghost of Christmas Present in A Christmas Carol?

Write about:

• *how Dickens presents the Ghost of Christmas Present in this extract*
• *how Dickens presents the Ghost of Christmas Present in the novel as a whole.*

[30 Marks] (AO1 = 12; AO2 = 12; AO3 = 6)

(50 Minutes Total = 40 Minutes Writing + 10 Minutes Reading Extract/Making Notes/Planning)

(600 Words Maximum per Essay = 15 Words per Minute)

Dickens presents the "Ghost of Christmas Present" in this extract as "...a jolly Giant, glorious to see;". The generous, vibrant nature of this Ghost is reflected in its welcoming manner towards Scrooge. "'Come in!' exclaimed the Ghost. 'Come in! and know me better, man!'" The word 'exclaimed' illustrates the passionate nature of the Ghost. His invitation to 'know me better' reflects its desire to engage with Scrooge. Scrooge is humbler in the presence of this "Spirit", as he "...entered timidly, and hung his head before this Spirit.". The ghost's welcoming nature is again demonstrated when it states "I am the Ghost of Christmas Present," and then, "Look upon me." The Ghost is presented by Dickens as unable to be contained in any way, in actions or appearance, "...its capacious breast was bare, as if disdaining to be warded or concealed by any artifice." In direct contrast to the indistinct, opaque "Ghost of Christmas Past", the "Ghost of Christmas Present" is entirely distinct and transparent. "Its dark brown curls were long and free; free as its genial face, its sparkling eye, its open hand, its cheery voice,". The adjectives that Dickens uses are complimentary and present an expansive and 'cheery' character. Dickens also uses contrasting imagery through the lines "...an antique scabbard; but no sword was in it, and the ancient sheath was eaten up with rust". This conveys the ghost's non-violent demeanour, as he has no 'sword' and the 'sheath' has been unused for a considerable amount of time, '...eaten up with rust.'

Following this extract, Scrooge is willing to learn any lessons that the "Ghost of Christmas Present" is willing to provide, "...if you have aught to teach me, let me profit by it." Dickens presents the "Ghost of Christmas Present" throughout the rest of the novel as showing Scrooge many visions from around the world on Christmas Day. Before witnessing the scene of celebration at the Cratchit family home, the Ghost once more demonstrates his kind and generous nature as "...the Spirit smiled, and stopped to bless Bob Cratchit's dwelling with the sprinkling of his torch." The sight of Tiny Tim saddens Scrooge and he asks "...with an interest he had never felt before, 'tell me if Tiny Tim will live.'" And the Ghost answers honestly and frankly, reflecting the words Scrooge had previously spoken, "If he be like to die, he had better do it, and decrease the surplus population" at which, "Scrooge bent before the Ghost's rebuke, and trembling cast his eyes upon the ground." The Ghost shows him two "ragged, scowling, wolfish;" children cowering under its cloak. They are called "Ignorance" and "Want" and the Ghost prophetically states that all will suffer unless the lessons of both generosity and tolerance are learned. When Scrooge enquires as to the children's welfare, the honesty and frankness of the Ghost is further exemplified as the Ghost again turns Scrooge's words back upon him "Are there no prisons? ...Are there no workhouses?"

Dickens presents the "Ghost of Christmas Present" as a pivotal character that drives the plot. The arrival of the "Ghost of Christmas Present" is a dramatic and structurally significant moment in the novella. There is dramatic irony also in how the Ghost twice reflects Scrooge's callous words back to him. In terms of its dramatic context, the spectacle of the presentation of the Ghost would have been enjoyed during the time of Dickens and is enjoyed contemporarily too. Dickens presents the character of the "Ghost of Christmas Present" as emblematic of his own belief; that the celebration of a traditional Christmas can help to restore social harmony.

(600 words)

By Joseph Anthony Campbell

A CHRISTMAS CAROL SIXTH ESSAY – TINY TIM

Read the following extract from Chapter 3 of <u>A Christmas Carol</u> and then answer the question that follows.

In this extract, the Ghost of Christmas Present shows Scrooge the Cratchit family home at Christmas.

...and Tiny Tim upon his shoulder. Alas for Tiny Tim, he bore a little crutch, and had his limbs supported by an iron frame!

"Why, where's our Martha?" cried Bob Cratchit, looking round.

"Not coming," said Mrs. Cratchit.

5 "Not coming!" said Bob, with a sudden declension in his high spirits; for he had been Tim's blood horse all the way from church, and had come home rampant. "Not coming upon Christmas Day!"

Martha didn't like to see him disappointed, if it were only in joke; so she came out prematurely from behind the closet door, and ran into his arms, while the two young 10 Cratchits hustled Tiny Tim, and bore him off into the wash-house, that he might hear the pudding singing in the copper.

"And how did little Tim behave?" asked Mrs. Cratchit, when she had rallied Bob on his credulity, and Bob had hugged his daughter to his heart's content.

"As good as gold," said Bob, "and better. Somehow he gets thoughtful, sitting by 15 himself so much, and thinks the strangest things you ever heard. He told me, coming home, that he hoped the people saw him in the church, because he was a

24

cripple, and it might be pleasant to them to remember upon Christmas Day, who made lame beggars walk, and blind men see."

Bob's voice was tremulous when he told them this, and trembled more when he said *20* that Tiny Tim was growing strong and hearty.

His active little crutch was heard upon the floor, and back came Tiny Tim before another word was spoken, escorted by his brother and sister to his stool before the fire; ...

Starting with this extract, how does Dickens present Tiny Tim in __A Christmas Carol__?

Write about:

• *how Dickens presents Tiny Tim in this extract*
• *how Dickens presents Tiny Tim in the novel as a whole.*

[30 Marks] (AO1 = 12; AO2 = 12; AO3 = 6)

(50 Minutes Total = 40 Minutes Writing + 10 Minutes Reading Extract/Making Notes/Planning)

(600 Words Maximum per Essay = 15 Words per Minute)

In this extract, Scrooge and the readers are introduced to the character of Tiny Tim, as his father Bob Cratchit carries "Tiny Tim upon his shoulder." Dickens uses a strong narrative voice throughout the novella. Dickens states, "Alas for Tiny Tim, he bore a little crutch, and had his limbs supported by an iron frame!" Tiny Tim is disabled yet despite his physical difficulties, he is a positive and generous child. Tiny Tim is both loved and supported by his family as shown in the following line, "...the two young Cratchits hustled Tiny Tim... that he might hear the pudding singing in the copper." The siblings considerately wish for him to enjoy the traditional delights of their family Christmas. Dickens also conveys that Tiny Tim is an exceptionally thoughtful, selfless child when Bob Cratchit states, "Somehow he gets thoughtful," and that Tiny Tim

"...hoped the people saw him in the church, ...it might be pleasant to them to remember upon Christmas Day, who made lame beggars walk, and blind men see." Tiny Tim thinks not of his own suffering and hopes that others will think of Jesus and that 'it might be pleasant to them'. Bob Cratchit loves his son dearly as "Bob's voice was tremulous when he told them this,". Perhaps Bob cannot face the true extent of his son's dire condition and the prospect of losing his child as he says to his wife that "...Tiny Tim was growing strong and hearty" and his voice "trembled more". Dickens exemplifies the belonging Tiny Tim experiences as he is "...escorted... to his stool before the fire; ..." as this is 'his stool'. Through the character of Tiny Tim in this extract, Dickens presents the importance of love and family in line with the Christmas tradition.

Dickens presents Tiny Tim in the novel as a whole as an extremely kind child. When Bob Cratchit proposes a toast at the Christmas dinner table, Tiny Tim adapts the toast to includes everyone. "God bless us every one!" Tiny Tim is kind and able to offer love to all of humanity. In contrast, when we are introduced to Scrooge, his behaviour and actions are diametrically opposed to Tiny Tim who exemplifies kindness, compassion and forgiveness and always thinks of others. Later, when we are shown Tiny Tim's death in the future, Bob remembers his son as a patient child "...when we recollect how patient and how mild he was". Bob's "little, little child;" is remembered fondly for his good qualities, and Bob says that the family "... shall not quarrel easily among ourselves and forget poor Tiny Tim in doing it." Dickens emotively states through the narrator; "Spirit of Tiny Tim, thy childish essence was from God!"

Dickens was moved by the plight of poor children in his lifetime. He witnessed children working in appalling conditions and the immense suffering of the half-starved, illiterate street children in London. He also experienced much suffering as a child himself and the character of Tiny Tim may be based on his nephew Henry who was a disabled boy and five at the time "A Christmas Carol" was written. Tiny Tim also allowed Dickens to present his metaphorical message of the need for charity towards the nation's poor children. At the end of the novella, we learn that Scrooge becomes like "a second father" to Tiny Tim. Tiny Tim is presented by Dickens as a pivotal character that drives the plot and this is further exemplified in the very last line of the novella, when Dickens states, "And so, as Tiny Tim observed, God bless Us, Every One!"

(600 words)

By Joseph Anthony Campbell

A CHRISTMAS CAROL SEVENTH ESSAY – THE CRATCHIT FAMILY AND THE STRUGGLES OF THE POOR

Read the following extract from Chapter 3 of <u>A Christmas Carol</u> and then answer the question that follows.

In this extract, the Ghost of Christmas Present shows Scrooge the Cratchit family's Christmas celebrations.

Oh, a wonderful pudding! Bob Cratchit said, and calmly too, that he regarded it as the greatest success achieved by Mrs. Cratchit since their marriage. Mrs. Cratchit said that now the weight was off her mind, she would confess she had had her doubts about the quantity of flour.
5 Everybody had something to say about it, but nobody said or thought it was at all a small pudding for a large family. It would have been flat heresy to do so. Any Cratchit would have blushed to hint at such a thing. At last the dinner was all done, the cloth was cleared, the hearth swept, and the fire made up. The compound in the jug being tasted, and
10 considered perfect, apples and oranges were put upon the table, and a shovel-full of chestnuts on the fire. Then all the Cratchit family drew

round the hearth, in what Bob Cratchit called a circle, meaning half a one; and at Bob Cratchit's elbow stood the family display of glass. Two tumblers, and a custard-cup without a handle.

15 These held the hot stuff from the jug, however, as well as golden goblets would have done; and Bob served it out with beaming looks, while the chestnuts on the fire sputtered and cracked noisily. Then Bob proposed:

"A Merry Christmas to us all, my dears. God bless us!"

Which all the family re-echoed.

20 "God bless us every one!" said Tiny Tim, the last of all.

He sat very close to his father's side upon his little stool. Bob held his withered little hand in his, as if he loved the child, and wished to keep him by his side, and dreaded that he might be taken from him.

Starting with this extract, explore how Dickens uses the Cratchit family to show the struggles of the poor.

Write about:

• *how Dickens presents the Cratchit family in this extract*
• *how Dickens uses the Cratchit family to show the struggles of the poor in the novel as a whole.*

[30 Marks] (AO1 = 12; AO2 = 12; AO3 = 6)

(50 Minutes Total = 40 Minutes Writing + 10 Minutes Reading Extract/Making Notes/Planning)

(600 Words Maximum per Essay = 15 Words per Minute)

In this extract, Dickens presents the Cratchit family's Christmas celebrations through a strong narrative voice that comments on the characters and through Dickens's highly descriptive language he creates a vivid representation of place and setting. The

Cratchits make the best of their limited means and their cheerful celebrations despite their obvious hardships endears them to the readers. The Cratchits are part of the poorer working classes of Victorian London and their plight is detailed in this extract yet Dickens also explores the importance of love and family through the Cratchits.

In this extract, the family's gratitude and appreciation for what they have is reflected in their appreciation of the "pudding". "Oh, a wonderful pudding! Bob Cratchit said" with the exclamatory remark expressing his joy and "Everybody had something to say about it," yet "...nobody said or thought it was at all a small pudding for a large family". Later in the extract, there is a description of the "family display of glass" which consists of "Two tumblers, and a custard-cup" and that this cup is, "without a handle". Yet, although the Cratchit family's poverty is accentuated by their meagre 'display of glass' it is fully functional and fit for purpose as, "These held the hot stuff from the jug, however, as well as golden goblets would have done". This symbolises perhaps that the love and the contentment that they have with one another on this Christmas day eliminates the need for more material possessions which would ultimately prove unnecessary anyway, as their meagre glass collection performs 'as well as golden goblets'. Dickens uses the narrative voice to describe how "Bob served it out with beaming looks" – which illustrates Bob's contentment through being surrounded by his family. The warmth 'beaming' from his face is reflected and reciprocated back to him. This is in clear contrast to the presentation of Scrooge in Stave I who is "...secret, and self-contained, and solitary as an oyster." Bob's love for Tiny Tim is conveyed as, "Bob held his withered little hand in his" and "wished to keep him by his side" as he fears an impending reality "and dreaded that he might be taken from him". The language used here suggests the strength of feeling that Bob has for Tiny Tim and mirrors the themes of poverty and the Cratchit's lack of means to prevent Tiny Tim from suffering an early, premature death.

Mrs Cratchit later describes Scrooge as an "odious, stingy, hard, unfeeling man" and the narrator states that he is the "Ogre of the family". Scrooge, as Bob Cratchit's employer, increases the struggles of the poor Cratchit family. Following Scrooge's later transformation, he states to Bob Cratchit, that he will "endeavour to assist your struggling family". Dickens' metaphorical message in this novella highlights what could be possible if the wealthy endeavoured to help the poor, as Scrooge is not a human being with mental processes separate from those of the author.

Dickens believed that the staging of Christmas in each family might help to restore social harmony. However, for the Cratchits and many in Victorian society, wealth inequality was a brutal reality. The novella's thematic elements also intertwine in complex ways. The themes of wealth and injustice are clear comments by Dickens as regards the inequalities of wealth distribution in Victorian England. Tiny Tim also reflects the issues of childhood illness and inaccessibility to Victorian medicine. Although there is perhaps a contrasting contemporary reception to Dickens novella compared to a modern reception, the themes of wealth inequality and inaccessibility to appropriate medical care is more prevalent today than Dickens would perhaps have hoped.

(600 words)

A CHRISTMAS CAROL EIGHTH ESSAY – THE THEMES OF POVERTY AND SOCIAL INJUSTICE

Read the following extract from Chapter 3 of <u>A Christmas Carol</u> and then answer the question that follows.

In this extract, Scrooge's time with the Ghost of Christmas Present is coming to an end.

From the foldings of its robe, it brought two children; wretched, abject, frightful, hideous, miserable. They knelt down at its feet, and clung upon the outside of its garment.

"Oh, Man, look here! Look, look, down here!" exclaimed the Ghost.

5 They were a boy and a girl. Yellow, meagre, ragged, scowling, wolfish; but prostrate, too, in their humility. Where graceful youth should have filled their features out, and touched them with its freshest tints, a stale and shrivelled hand, like that of age, had pinched, and twisted them, and pulled them into shreds. Where angels might have sat enthroned, devils lurked, and glared out menacing. No change, no degradation, no

10 perversion of humanity, in any grade, through all the mysteries of wonderful creation, has monsters half so horrible and dread.

Scrooge started back, appalled. Having them shown to him in this way, he tried to say they were fine children, but the words choked themselves, rather than be parties to a lie of such enormous magnitude.

15 "Spirit, are they yours?" Scrooge could say no more.

"They are Man's," said the Spirit, looking down upon them. "And they cling to me, appealing from their fathers. This boy is Ignorance. This girl is Want. Beware them both, and all of their degree, but most of all beware this boy, for on his brow I see that written which is Doom, unless the writing be erased. Deny it!" cried the Spirit, stretching out

20 its hand towards the city. "Slander those who tell it ye. Admit it for your factious purposes, and make it worse. And abide the end."

"Have they no refuge or resource?" cried Scrooge.

"Are there no prisons?" said the Spirit, turning on him for the last time with his own words. "Are there no workhouses?"

Starting with this extract, how does Dickens present the themes of poverty and social injustice in _A Christmas Carol_?

Write about:

• how Dickens presents the themes of poverty and social injustice in this extract
• how Dickens presents the themes of poverty and social injustice in the novel as a whole.

[30 Marks] (AO1 = 12; AO2 = 12; AO3 = 6)

(50 Minutes Total = 40 Minutes Writing + 10 Minutes Reading Extract/Making Notes/Planning)

(600 Words Maximum per Essay = 15 Words per Minute)

Dickens presents the themes of poverty and social injustice in this extract through two emaciated children named "Ignorance" and "Want". The children are an emblematic representation of the poor children of Victorian society and Dickens' language in describing them is highly descriptive and creates a vivid sense of their desperate condition, "...abject, frightful, hideous". The children are brought forward by the

"Ghost of Christmas Present" and "...clung upon the outside of its garment". The children highlight the unfairness of Victorian society through Dickens' presentation and description of their desperate state of lack, "They were a boy and girl. Yellow, meagre, ragged, scowling, wolfish". They metaphorically represent the repercussions of greed. This is heightened further through Dickens' presentation of their physical state, "...a stale and shrivelled hand, like that of age, had pinched, and twisted them". The children are 'pinched' and 'twisted' which is diametrically opposed to how children should be when "graceful youth should have filled their features out" and Dickens further states, "Where angels might have sat enthroned, devils lurked,". The children's deep, desperate poverty and the social injustice which has created it, leads Dickens to present fearful images in this extract, "No change, no degradation, no perversion of humanity, ...has monsters half so horrible and dread." In this extract, the 'Ghost' states of the children that "They are Man's,". The 'Ghost' then prophetically and apocalyptically states, "Most of all beware this boy, for on his brow I see that written which is Doom, unless the writing be erased." Dickens is stating here that unless generosity and tolerance replace social injustice and the poverty it inevitably leads to, that 'Doom' will be the result, in this dramatic and structurally significant part of the novella.

Initially, Dickens presents the themes of poverty and social injustice in the novel, when Scrooge is asked by the "portly gentlemen" to help the "Poor and Destitute" of society. Scrooge refuses to give money. In Victorian times, poor children would be sent to live in workhouses and Scrooge insists that prisons and workhouses should deal with the destitute, even callously stating, "'If they would rather die,' said Scrooge, 'they had better do it, and decrease the surplus population.'" Through Scrooge's selfishness and self-centredness Dickens highlights the injustice of wealth distribution in Victorian society. This inequality is such, that the poor even steal and sell the belongings of the dead. The thieves of stave four, show how people were driven by poverty and social inequality to steal from the dead. The thieves are even aware that they have to go to "old Joe" to sell their stolen property; which shows how this was a part of normal life for them. However, Scrooge's selfish life affects not only himself but others, as they feel justified in dividing up Scrooge's belongings, with the woman stating, "Every person has a right to take care of themselves. He always did."

In a social and historical context, Dickens felt strongly that Victorian society ignored the poverty and social injustice prevalent throughout the country. In his lifetime, Dickens was angered by the intense suffering that he witnessed of children working in appalling conditions and in the schools that were filled with half-starved, illiterate street children. The two children of 'Ignorance' and 'Want' are presented by Dickens as a warning of the terrible realities that are created throughout society by the widespread 'Ignorance' of the devastating 'Want' existing amongst its' poor. The themes of poverty and social injustice permeate throughout the novella and clearly delineate the inequalities of wealth distribution that existed in Victorian England and also has relevance for modern-day readers also.

(600 words)

By Joseph Anthony Campbell

A CHRISTMAS CAROL NINTH ESSAY – BOB CRATCHIT

Read the following extract from Chapter 4 of <u>A Christmas Carol</u> and then answer the question that follows.

In this extract the Ghost of Christmas Yet to Come shows Scrooge a 'tenderness connected with a death.'

"I have known him walk with— I have known him walk with Tiny Tim upon his shoulder, very fast indeed."

"And so have I," cried Peter. "Often."

"And so have I," exclaimed another. So had all.

5 "But he was very light to carry," she resumed, intent upon her work, "and his father loved him so, that it was no trouble: no trouble. And there is your father at the door!"

She hurried out to meet him; and little Bob in his comforter— he had need of it, poor fellow— came in. His tea was ready for him on the hob, and they all tried who should help him to it most. Then the two young Cratchits got upon his knees and laid, each *10* child a little cheek, against his face, as if they said, "Don't mind it, father. Don't be grieved!"

Bob was very cheerful with them, and spoke pleasantly to all the family. He looked at the work upon the table, and praised the industry and speed of Mrs. Cratchit and the girls. They would be done long before Sunday, he said.

15 "Sunday! You went to-day, then, Robert?" said his wife.

"Yes, my dear," returned Bob. "I wish you could have gone. It would have done you good to see how green a place it is. But you'll see it often. I promised him that I would walk there on a Sunday. My little, little child!" cried Bob. "My little child!"

He broke down all at once. He couldn't help it. If he could have helped it, he and his **20** child would have been farther apart perhaps than they were.

He left the room, and went up-stairs into the room above, which was lighted cheerfully, and hung with Christmas. There was a chair set close beside the child, and there were signs of some one having been there, lately. Poor Bob sat down in it, and when he had thought a little and composed himself, he kissed the little face. He was reconciled to

25 what had happened, and went down again quite happy.

Starting with this extract, how does Dickens present Bob Cratchit in <u>*A Christmas Carol?*</u>

Write about:

• *how Dickens presents Bob Cratchit in this extract*
• *how Dickens presents Bob Cratchit in the novel as a whole.*

[30 Marks] (AO1 = 12; AO2 = 12; AO3 = 6)

(50 Minutes Total = 40 Minutes Writing + 10 Minutes Reading Extract/Making Notes/Planning)

(600 Words Maximum per Essay = 15 Words per Minute)

Bob Cratchit is a pivotal character that drives the plot. In this extract, Dickens sets the scene when Mrs. Cratchit states proudly, "I have known him walk with Tiny Tim upon his shoulder, very fast indeed". We also obtain an insight into Bob's caring nature when Mrs. Cratchit states "and his father loved him so, that it was no trouble: no trouble." The love Bob's children have for him is evident also when the "two young

Cratchits ...laid, each child a little cheek, against his face, as if they said, 'Don't mind it, father. Don't be grieved!'". Despite the grievous loss he has suffered, "Bob was very cheerful with them, and spoke pleasantly to all the family." Bob does not react angrily or vent his anger upon his family, he is both mature and balanced in his emotions. He also expresses his sensitivity and tenderness. "'My little, little child!' cried Bob. 'My little child!'". The repetition and reinforcement of the word 'little' here adds to this poignant moment. The narrator opines of Bob Cratchit that "If he could have helped it, he and his child would have been farther apart perhaps than they were." As readers, we feel sympathy for Bob and here, we can discern his sensitivity and his deep love for his son, shown here through his grief. Yet, Bob regains his composure and accepts what has happened to his young son by the end of the extract as "he kissed the little face. He was reconciled to what had happened, and went down again quite happy." Bob's actions here endear him further to the readers.

In the novel as a whole, Dickens presents Bob Cratchit as a man who has humility, integrity, a strong work ethic and a deep love for his family. Bob Cratchit is Scrooge's clerk and works in unpleasant conditions to the best of his ability with obedience and equanimity, i.e., "The clerk put on his white comforter, and tried to warm himself at the candle;". Later, when the Ghost of Christmas Present takes Scrooge to visit the Cratchits on Christmas Day, we observe Bob Cratchit carrying his ill son "Tiny Tim upon his shoulder," and Bob later raises a toast to Scrooge for providing the feast, "'I'll give you Mr. Scrooge, the Founder of the Feast!'". This shows Bob's generosity of spirit and his gratitude. However, he is fearful of Scrooge when he arrives late in Stave V "'It's only once a year, sir,' pleaded Bob". Dickens use of 'pleaded' here highlights the power dynamic that exists between Scrooge and his clerk; yet Bob also welcomes Scrooge's transformation and help at the very end of the novella.

In a social and historical context, the life of a Victorian clerk was notoriously dull. They often spent long hours working for the benefits of others. Dickens works featured many clerks who had difficult, drab lives. However, the character of Bob Cratchit would have been appreciated by Dickens contemporaries. Victorian ideas about men and masculinity possibly contrast with our modern notions yet Bob Cratchit is presented as a sensitive and caring family man. Bob Cratchit's reaction to his young son 'Tiny Tim' dying perhaps highlights contextual differences in terms of potentially different reactions over time. Child mortality is much lower now and there is more access to healthcare for the lower classes. Therefore, Bob's acceptance and reconcilement with the potentially avoidable death of his young son would perhaps be considered a grave injustice in a modern context. Overall, the sensitivity and compassion of the character of Bob Cratchit is perhaps also somewhat drawn from Dickens himself.

(600 words)

By Joseph Anthony Campbell

A CHRISTMAS CAROL TENTH ESSAY – SCROOGE'S FEARS

Read the following extract from Chapter 4 of <u>A Christmas Carol</u> and then answer the question that follows.

In this extract, Scrooge meets the Ghost of Christmas Yet to Come.

The Phantom slowly, gravely, silently, approached. When it came near him, Scrooge bent down upon his knee; for in the very air through which this Spirit moved it seemed to scatter gloom and mystery.

It was shrouded in a deep black garment, which concealed its head, its face, its
5 form, and left nothing of it visible save one outstretched hand. But for this it would have been difficult to detach its figure from the night, and separate it from the darkness by which it was surrounded.

He felt that it was tall and stately when it came beside him, and that its mysterious presence filled him with a solemn dread. He knew no more, for the
10 Spirit neither spoke nor moved.

"I am in the presence of the Ghost of Christmas Yet to Come?" said Scrooge.

The Spirit answered not, but pointed onward with its hand.

"You are about to show me shadows of the things that have not happened, but will happen in the time before us," Scrooge pursued. "Is that so, Spirit?" The
15 upper portion of the garment was contracted for an instant in its folds, as if the Spirit had inclined its head. That was the only answer he received.

Although well used to ghostly company by this time, Scrooge feared the silent

shape so much that his legs trembled beneath him, and he found that he could hardly stand when he prepared to follow it. The Spirit paused a moment, as
20 observing his condition, and giving him time to recover.

But Scrooge was all the worse for this. It thrilled him with a vague uncertain horror, to know that behind the dusky shroud, there were ghostly eyes intently fixed upon him, while he, though he stretched his own to the utmost, could see nothing but a spectral hand and one great heap of black.

25 "Ghost of the Future!" he exclaimed, "I fear you more than any spectre I have seen. But as I know your purpose is to do me good, and as I hope to live to be another man from what I was, I am prepared to bear you company, and do it with a thankful heart. Will you not speak to me?"

Starting with this extract, explore how Dickens presents Scrooge's fears in _A Christmas Carol_.

Write about:

• how Dickens presents what Scrooge is frightened of in this extract
• how Dickens presents Scrooge's fears in the novel as a whole.

[30 Marks] (AO1 = 12; AO2 = 12; AO3 = 6)

(50 Minutes Total = 40 Minutes Writing + 10 Minutes Reading Extract/Making Notes/Planning)

(600 Words Maximum per Essay = 15 Words per Minute)

Dickens presents Scrooge's fear of the "Phantom" in this extract, through the language he uses to present its appearance and actions, "...the Spirit neither spoke nor moved." The spirit's silence is complete and it can also barely be observed, "...nothing of it visible save one outstretched hand". The 'Phantom' is also "shrouded" which brings to mind images of death and is emblematic of what the Phantom will show

Scrooge during their time together. The Phantom is silent, dark and ominous yet, the line "...it seemed to scatter gloom and mystery", presents a duality and seeming contradiction in Dickens language as 'mystery' has fewer dark connotations than 'gloom'. The fearful image of the Phantom intensifies Scrooge's fears and "filled him with a solemn dread". Dickens presents Scrooge's fearful response as he feels "...a vague uncertain horror," and Dickens states that "Scrooge feared the silent shape so much that his legs trembled beneath him," and that Scrooge "could hardly stand". Scrooge even emphatically states, "I fear you more than any spectre I have seen." Scrooge's honesty here endears him to the readers in this dramatically and structurally significant moment in the novella. Formerly, Scrooge feared poverty and despite being rich, his fears remained.

Dickens presents Scrooge's fears in the novel as a whole as the three ghosts show Scrooge the past, present and future. However, Scrooge fears all of the ghosts, including that of Marley, his former business partner. As Scrooge is visited by Marley, Dickens states that, "Scrooge trembled more and more." When Scrooge is visited by the first Spirit, the "Ghost of Christmas Past", he states, "'I am mortal,' Scrooge remonstrated, 'and liable to fall'" and when he first meets the "Ghost of Christmas Present", it is stated in the novella that "He was not the dogged Scrooge he had been; and though the Spirit's eyes were clear and kind, he did not like to meet them." Dickens presents Scrooge's fears during the appearance of each ghost and the intensification of Scrooge's fears culminates with the "Ghost of Christmas Yet to Come". This 'Phantom' shows Scrooge a vision of businessmen who are indifferent to the plight of a dead man and then moves onwards to a scene of people stealing the belongings of this deceased man. Finally, Scrooge is shown a tombstone engraved with his name and he realises that he is the dead man of the visions. Earlier also, as he witnesses scenes of family celebration, he realises what he is missing out on in his life. Scrooge therefore promises to change his ways if he can avoid this solitary, lonely death.

In Victorian times, there was a tradition of reading and telling ghost stories at Christmas. Dickens use of ghosts in the novella elicits fear in Scrooge and in the reader also. The dramatic context and spectacle of the supernatural would have been enjoyed during the time of Dickens and there may be a possibly contrasting contemporary reception with that of a modern reception, as belief in ghosts may be less widespread in a modern context than at the time Dickens wrote the novella. Dickens explores features of the genre of Gothic literature, of which our more modern equivalent is ghost and horror stories. Dickens also provides several small, thematic elements that intertwine in a complex way through abrupt shifts from comedy to tragedy. The contrast of light and dark also acts as an intertwining metaphor throughout the novella and Scrooge's fears are presented by Dickens as a motivating force for his transformation. Ultimately, Dickens presents Scrooge's redemption and spiritual re-education through his willingness and courage to change.

(600 words)

A CHRISTMAS CAROL ELEVENTH ESSAY – THE GHOST OF CHRISTMAS YET TO COME

Read the following extract from Chapter 4 of <u>A Christmas Carol</u> and then answer the question that follows.

In this extract, it is the end of Scrooge's time with the Ghost of Christmas Yet to Come.

The Spirit stood among the graves, and pointed down to One. He advanced towards it trembling. The Phantom was exactly as it had been, but he dreaded that he saw new meaning in its solemn shape.

"Before I draw nearer to that stone to which you point," said Scrooge, "answer me one

5 question. Are these the shadows of the things that Will be, or are they shadows of things that May be, only?"

Still the Ghost pointed downward to the grave by which it stood.

"Men's courses will foreshadow certain ends, to which, if persevered in, they must lead," said Scrooge. "But if the courses be departed from, the ends will change. Say it

10 is thus with what you show me."

The Spirit was immovable as ever.

Scrooge crept towards it, trembling as he went; and following the finger, read upon the stone of the neglected grave his own name, EBENEZER SCROOGE.

"Am I that man who lay upon the bed?" he cried, upon his knees.

15 The finger pointed from the grave to him, and back again.

"No, Spirit! Oh no, no!"

The finger still was there.

"Spirit!" he cried, tight clutching at its robe, "hear me. I am not the man I was. I will not be the man I must have been but for this intercourse. Why show me this, if I am

20 past all hope?"

For the first time the hand appeared to shake.

"Good Spirit," he pursued, as down upon the ground he fell before it: "Your nature intercedes for me, and pities me. Assure me that I yet may change these shadows you have shown me, by an altered life."

25 The kind hand trembled.

"I will honour Christmas in my heart, and try to keep it all the year. I will live in the Past, the Present, and the Future. The Spirits of all Three shall strive within me. I will not shut out the lessons that they teach. Oh, tell me I may sponge away the writing on this stone!"

Starting with this extract, how does Dickens present the Ghost of Christmas Yet to Come in _A Christmas Carol_?

Write about:

• how Dickens presents the Ghost of Christmas Yet to Come in this extract
• how Dickens presents the Ghost of Christmas Yet to Come in the novel as a whole.

[30 Marks] (AO1 = 12; AO2 = 12; AO3 = 6)

(50 Minutes Total = 40 Minutes Writing + 10 Minutes Reading Extract/Making Notes/Planning)

(600 Words Maximum per Essay = 15 Words per Minute)

Dickens presents a build-up of dramatic tension prior to this extract, which begins with the powerful image of, "The Spirit stood among the graves,". Dickens presents the "Ghost of Christmas Yet to Come" in this extract, initially through this fearful image. The 'Ghost' is ominous, as it "pointed down to One"; a tombstone engraved with Scrooge's name. The 'Ghost' points and does not move until it is obeyed. Scrooge has to assess what the 'Ghost' is communicating to him as the 'Ghost' remains unchanged in its demeanour, "The Phantom was exactly as it had been, but he dreaded that he saw new meaning in its solemn shape." The 'Ghost' silently demands that Scrooge pay attention, "Still the Ghost pointed downward to the grave by which it stood." Dickens presents the 'Spirit' as unrelenting and implacable, "The Spirit was immovable as ever." Dickens repeats the word, 'pointed' again, when he states, "The finger pointed from the grave to him, and back again." This use of repetition reinforces the immovable nature of the 'Ghost' as it remains unmoved by Scrooge's pleas for a chance to change his fate, "The finger still was there." The absence of language from the 'Ghost' highlights the power dynamic between it and Scrooge; the 'Ghost' does not have to speak to be obeyed. However, Dickens displays the Ghost's merciful nature in this extract, as after further determined and more emotionally heightened pleas from Scrooge, "For the first time the hand appeared to shake." This clemency is exemplified by the following line, "The kind hand trembled." There is a duality presented by Dickens here, through the description of 'The kind hand' attributed to a 'Spirit' that is presented as being largely synonymous with death. Dickens' highly evocative language in this extract creates a vivid sense of the 'Ghost of Christmas Yet to Come' through this dramatic and structurally significant part of the novella.

Dickens presents the 'Ghost of Christmas Yet to Come' in the novel as a whole, as silent, dark and ominous. He describes it as "...a solemn Phantom, draped and hooded, coming, like a mist along the ground." Haunting, frightening and eerie "...the Spirit neither spoke nor moved." It can barely be observed, and it is "shrouded" which brings to mind images of death and is emblematic of what the 'Phantom' will show Scrooge during their time together. Dickens presents the 'Ghost' as instilling terror deep within Scrooge and it provides the realisation of Scrooge's deepest fears throughout their time together. The 'Ghost' glides along and leads Scrooge through episodes relating to "Death." It shows Scrooge scenes associated with an unnamed man's death and takes him to a "fearful place", a place where there is "emotion caused by this man's death" and to "some tenderness connected with a death"; culminating with the lonely, neglected, gravestone of "EBENEZER SCROOGE". However, ultimately, the Spirit shows him all this for his benefit.

During the time that Dickens wrote this novella, ghost stories were traditionally told at Christmas. Therefore, the supernatural would have been greatly enjoyed during Victorian times. There may be some differences contextually in terms of how a modern audience would react to ghosts. Dickens also presents the unusual nature of the relationship between the "Ghost of Christmas Yet to Come" and Scrooge, especially when contrasted with the presentation of the "Ghost of Christmas Present" for example. Yet, despite the Ghost's ominous presence, it bestows mercy upon Scrooge. The 'Ghost' represents both justice and mercy, throughout its interactions with Scrooge. This seeming duality of kindness and darkness is presented by Dickens as an intertwining metaphor throughout the novella.

(600 words)

A CHRISTMAS CAROL TWELFTH ESSAY – SCROOGE'S TRANSFORMATION

Read the following extract from Chapter 5 of <u>A Christmas Carol</u> and then answer the question that follows.

In this extract, Scrooge has returned home after his night with the Spirits.

"I don't know what to do!" cried Scrooge, laughing and crying in the same breath; and making a perfect Laocoön of himself with his stockings. "I am as light as a feather, I am as happy as an angel, I am as merry as a schoolboy. I am as giddy as a drunken man. A merry Christmas to everybody! A happy New Year to all the world. Hallo here! Whoop!

5 Hallo!"

He had frisked into the sitting-room, and was now standing there: perfectly winded.

"There's the saucepan that the gruel was in!" cried Scrooge, starting off again, and going round the fireplace.

"There's the door, by which the Ghost of Jacob Marley entered! There's the corner where

10 the Ghost of Christmas Present, sat! There's the window where I saw the wandering Spirits! It's all right, it's all true, it all happened. Ha ha ha!"

Really, for a man who had been out of practice for so many years, it was a splendid laugh, a most illustrious laugh. The father of a long, long line of brilliant laughs!

"I don't know what day of the month it is!" said Scrooge. "I don't know how long I've
15 been among the Spirits. I don't know anything. I'm quite a baby. Never mind. I
don't care. I'd rather be a baby. Hallo! Whoop! Hallo here!"
He was checked in his transports by the churches ringing out the lustiest peals he had
ever heard. Clash, clang, hammer; ding, dong, bell. Bell, dong, ding; hammer, clang,
clash! Oh, glorious, glorious!
20 Running to the window, he opened it, and put out his head. No fog, no mist; clear,
bright, jovial, stirring, cold; cold, piping for the blood to dance to; Golden sunlight;
Heavenly sky; sweet fresh air; merry bells. Oh, glorious! Glorious!

Starting with this extract, how does Dickens show the transformation of Scrooge's
character in A __Christmas Carol__?

Write about:

• *how Dickens shows Scrooge's transformation in this extract*
• *how Dickens shows Scrooge's transformation from the beginning of the novella.*

[30 Marks] (AO1 = 12; AO2 = 12; AO3 = 6)

(50 Minutes Total = 40 Minutes Writing + 10 Minutes Reading Extract/Making
Notes/Planning)

(600 Words Maximum per Essay = 15 Words per Minute)

Dickens shows Scrooge's transformation in this extract as an emotional, joyous
Scrooge is "laughing and crying in the same breath" and "making a perfect Laocoön
of himself". Dickens is referring to a famous statue of a man in agony here and this
implies that Scrooge is struggling "with his stockings." Dickens uses joyful similes as
Scrooge states, "I am as light as a feather, I am as happy as an angel" and pronounces
exclamations of joy, "Whoop! Hallo!". The onomatopoeia of 'Whoop!' conveys a sense
of Scrooge's joy and reformation and brings to mind the character of Fezziwig and his

exclamations of "Hilli-ho," and "Chirrup." Scrooge's renewed zest for life is evidenced when he states, "A merry Christmas to everybody! A happy New Year to all the world" which is in stark contrast to his cold and dismissive "Good afternoon," when his nephew Fred bestowed the season's greetings upon him. Scrooge is grateful to remember that, "There's the window where I saw the wandering Spirits!" He also now has, "...a most illustrious laugh. The father of a long, long line of brilliant laughs!". Here, Dickens informs us that Scrooge's 'laugh' will be an integral part of his character. When Scrooge states, "I don't know anything. I'm quite a baby" this brings into mind stave 4 when he hears, "'And He took a child, and set him in the midst of them.'". This quote is from the New Testament and Dickens perhaps illustrates that he is now like 'a child' and appreciates all that he can observe and failed to notice before, such as, "Golden sunlight; Heavenly sky; sweet fresh air; merry bells." Dickens also uses repetition to reinforce Scrooge's newfound levels of appreciation and the deep transformation that he has experienced, "Oh, glorious! Glorious".

Dickens clearly conveys Scrooge's transformation from the beginning of the novella where Scrooge is described in Stave I, as a "...squeezing, wrenching, grasping, scraping, clutching, covetous, old sinner!". Dickens' use of adjectives here provides examples that heighten and emphasise how tightly Scrooge holds on to everything he has, as each adjective is connected with his hands and he is described as a "tight-fisted hand at the grindstone,". Dickens' language is highly descriptive here and creates a vivid sense of the miserly nature of Scrooge through both the use of emphatic statements and through comic references to Scrooge's characteristics. Dickens uses exclamatory marks to express that even the narrator is stupefied by Scrooge's miserly nature, 'Oh!' and also uses alliteration to describe Scrooge's isolated nature, "secret, and self-contained" and a simile, "solitary as an oyster." Scrooge's unapproachable nature is also conveyed in a further simile, "Hard and sharp as flint". It is evident that there is a clear duality between Scrooge in Stave 1 to when he is transformed in Stave 5.

Scrooge's journey of transformation is central to the novella. Scrooge is presented as a protean figure, always in a process of transformation; from when the ghost of Marley visits him. Scrooge begins the novella as a paradigm of self-interest and becomes a man who realises his own emotional depth and reflects honestly on the lost opportunities of his life. Scrooge endears himself to the readers and the dramatic context and spectacle of Scrooge's transformation would have been greatly enjoyed during the time that Dickens wrote the novella. The presentation of Scrooge's redemption and transformation in the final stave provides the reader with both hope and possibility. At the conclusion of the novella, Scrooge's transformation is complete and he has at last found contentment, for, "His own heart laughed: and that was quite enough for him."

(600 words)

ASSESSMENT OBJECTIVES

There are **four assessment objectives** assessed in each English Literature examination: **(no AO4 assessment for the 'A Christmas Carol' section) AO1, (12 Marks) AO2 (12 Marks) AO3 (6 Marks) and AO4 (4 marks for Spelling and Grammar).**

AO1 = Read, understand and respond to the text (**A Christmas Carol**) and the task set in the question. Use 4 to 6 quotations you may have memorised from the novella (or memorise those that I have provided in my answers in this book on various characters/themes in the novella).

AO2 = Analyse the language, form and structure used by a writer (**Dickens**) to create meanings and effects i.e., also mention '**Dickens**' 4 to 6 times or more in your answer and how he presents characters/themes and creates meanings and effects.

AO3 = is the understanding of the relationship between the ideas in the text and the context/time in which the text was written and the context within which the text is set.

AO4 = spell and punctuate with consistent accuracy, and consistently use vocabulary and sentence structures to achieve control of the meaning you are aiming to convey.

The Assessment Objectives are not provided in the examination itself. However, I have provided which assessment objectives are being assessed in the practice questions in this book. It is important to be aware of the structure of how the assessment objectives are allocated in each question of the exam in order to maximise your opportunities to obtain full marks in each question.

It is a good idea also to plan your answer before you begin writing it. A plan will mean you answer the question in an organised and sequenced manner. Your newfound understanding of the assessment objectives will also ensure you have met all of the required criteria.

TIMINGS

In the English Literature GCSE Paper 1 examination there are 60 marks to aim for in 1 hour and 40 minutes (100 minutes). Please allocate the correct words per minute per mark! Again, to re-iterate: The best approach is to spend 50 minutes on each question - 40 minutes writing and 10 minutes making notes, planning and checking your final answer for basic corrections at the end of the examination.

If you have extra time allocated to you, just change the calculation to accommodate the extra time you have i.e., if you have 25% extra time (= 50 minutes writing per question = 12 words per minute and 20 words per mark) and if you have 50% extra time (= 1 hour writing per question = 10 words per minute and 20 words per mark) also equals a 600-word essay for each section on Paper 1. Please **move on from the set question as soon as you have reached or are coming towards your time limit**. This ensures that you have excellent coverage of your whole exam and therefore attain a very good mark.

Similar to all the principles in this book, **you must apply and follow the correct timings for each question and stick to them throughout your exam to get an A star (Grade 9) in your English Literature examinations.** Without applying this principle in these examinations (and to a large extent all examinations) you cannot achieve the highest marks! **Apply all of the principles provided in this book to succeed!**

APPROXIMATE WORD COUNT PER QUESTION

Now that you know what is on each examination, how the assessment objectives are assessed and the time allocated for each type of question; we come to what would be considered the correct word count per mark for each question. The primary principle though is to spend the right amount of time on each question.

In the answers in this book, I have provided the maximum word count theoretically possible for each answer which works out at **15 words per minute and 20 words per mark and therefore this equals a 600-word essay for each section on Paper 1**. If your answer has quality, this gives you the very best chance of obtaining the highest marks in your English Literature exam. Obviously, it does not if you are waffling however. (Please remember to answer the question set and to move on in the time allocated.)

I am aware that some students can write faster than others but all should be able to write 10 words per minute and thus a 400-word essay in the time (if they have not been allocated extra time). This is where conciseness is important in your writing.

My students and readers have applied all of the techniques of the Quality Control System™ I am providing you with; to gain A stars (Grade 9's) in their examinations. You can replicate them by following the advice in this book.

Thank you for purchasing this book and best wishes for your examinations! Joseph

AUTHOR'S NOTE

This book will provide you with 12 crystal clear and accurate examples of 'A' star grade (Grade 9) AQA GCSE English Literature Paper 1 **'A Christmas Carol'** answers from the **'19th – century novel'** section of the new syllabus and enables students to achieve the same grade in their upcoming examinations.

I teach both GCSE and A level English and Psychology and I am a qualified and experienced teacher and tutor of over 18 years standing. I teach, write and provide independent tuition in central and west London.

The resources in this book WILL help you to get an A star (Grade/Level 9) in your GCSE English Literature examinations, as they have done and will continue to do so, for my students.

Best wishes,

Joseph

ABOUT THE AUTHOR

I graduated from the Universities of Liverpool and Leeds and I obtained first class honours in my teacher training.

I have taught and provided private tuition for over 18 years up to university level. I also write academic resources for the Times Educational Supplement.

My tuition students, and now, my readers, have been fortunate enough to attain places to study at Oxford, Cambridge and Imperial College, London and other Russell Group Universities. The students have done very well in their examinations. I hope and know that my English Literature books can enable you to take the next step on your academic journey.

Printed in Great Britain
by Amazon

79714597R00034